HANA HIGHWAY
MILE BY MILE
The Road to Hana & Beyond
Fourth Edition

**Researched &
Written by:**

John and Natasha Derrick

Hawaiian Style Organization LLC
www.HawaiianStyle.org

HANA HIGHWAY - MILE BY MILE
The Road to Hana & Beyond; Fourth Edition

Published by:
Hawaiian Style Organization LLC
PO BOX 965
Columbia, South Carolina 29202-0965
www.HawaiianStyle.org
Published 2007

ISBN-13: 978-0-9773880-9-7
ISBN-10: 0-9773880-9-3
Printed in the United States

Also available in electronic (eBook) format at: *www.HawaiianStyle.org*
Published 2007-2008
Printed in the United States

Language Note: Hawai'i's two official languages are Hawaiian and English. It is the only state in the U.S. with two official languages. In this guide we used both the English and Hawaiian names of places when possible. There are only 13 letters in the Hawaiian alphabet: A, E, H, I K, L, M, N, O, P, U, W and the 'okina ('). The okina is a glottal stop like the sound between the ohs in "oh-oh" and is considered a consonant. In order to clarify pronunciation, you will often see the glottal stop (') or 'okina used on words in this guide such as Hawai'i. Due to printing restrictions, we will not use the macron, which is found above stressed vowels in the Hawaiian language.

Photographs on pages 17, 25, 32, 33, 38, 40, 42, 43, and 45 taken by Forest and Kim Starr. These images are licensed under a Creative Commons Attribution 3.0 License, permitting sharing and adaptation with attribution.

All additional photographs taken by John and Natasha Derrick (2002-2005).

Cartography, map imagery and artwork by John Derrick.

TABLE OF CONTENTS

Hana Highway Introduction

CHAPTER 1
Highway 36 & Pa'ia Town

CHAPTER 2
Highway 360 - The Road to Hana

TABLE OF CONTENTS

CHAPTER 3
Highway 31 - Beyond Hana Town

CHAPTER 4
'Ohe'o Gulch & Kipahulu Area

CHAPTER 5
South Kipahulu, Mokulau & Kaupo

CHAPTER 6
Upcountry Maui, Kula & Highway 37

HIGHWAY MAPS
Hana, Pi'ilani & Kula Highway Maps

PREFACE
Highway to Heaven?

Imagine this: You get in your rental car one early morning (perhaps earlier than you'd like on your vacation) and you head out for this famous drive you've heard so much about. You can only hope the sunrise drive is worth it. As you reach the junction of Highway 36 and Highway 360 you begin to realize you're embarking on a journey unlike any you've ever taken. Before you are more than a 100 miles of undeveloped road and a landscape almost as pure and natural as it was a 1,000 years ago when the first Hawaiians arrived. And if you think you've seen beautiful drives, forget what you've seen, because the Hana Highway is perhaps the most pristine and jaw-dropping drive in all the world.

There are few words that can describe the cliffs cloaked in green, the lush valleys bursting with waterfalls more beautiful than you've ever seen. Its curves hug the coast and gaze over an ocean that stretches uninterrupted all the way to the Alaska coastline. Couple that with the black sand beaches (and some

This lookout near mile marker 14, with its view of the highway and Honomanu Bay, is one of the most famous of the drive. See page 28 for more details.

red ones too) and the multitude of trails, and the Hana Highway will reveal the island to you in a way you never imagined. Suddenly, the early rise seems so worth it - you only wish you had more time. Aloha to the Hana Highway and beyond on the island of Maui, Hawai'i.

When it comes to driving to Hana Town, it's the journey, not the destination, that is the main attraction. As you drive along the 52 miles of undeveloped road, with 56 one-lane bridges and 617 curves and turns, you will pass by the most breathtaking scenery on the face of the earth. It was literally a million years in the making.

You'll have to get up early to start this trip; 7 a.m. or earlier is best to get your start in Pa'ia town. An earlier morning means less traffic, and the more traffic you can avoid the more enjoyable your trip down the highway will be. If there is one complaint about the Hana Highway, it's almost always about the traffic. So avoid the rush, get started early, and you'll enjoy your trip significantly more.

Without any stops, it can take up to three hours to make the 52-mile journey to Hana. Some visitors and residents will try and do it in half that time. Don't let yourself be rushed. Just be sure to show some Aloha and pull over occasionally and let those by who are in a hurry. And don't forget that the journey

doesn't end in Hana; it continues well beyond the sleepy coastal town in the bay.

All in all, you can expect the drive described in this book to last about two full days. It'll really depend on how often you stop, which places you visit, and how much time you spend at each stop. The drive to Hana Town, with all the listed stops included, can take about a full day. The drive beyond Hana, including the 'Ohe'o Gulch, can easily take another day. To keep from driving any portion of the highway more than once, we recommend booking a room in Hana Town for a night (or more). Staying over at least one night will make your experience in east Maui feel far less rushed.

Along the journey there are several charming roadside stands selling refreshing tropical fruit, snacks and beautiful island flowers. But remember that you can't take fruit or the flowers out of Hawai'i, so only buy what you plan to enjoy while in the islands. If you want to take a bit of aloha home with you, you'll find that the Kahului airport stores sell plenty of ready-for-takeoff pineapples and other goods.

We recommend picking up a foam cooler, ice, canned beverages and some snacks/small meals before heading out. It also is good to bring along toilet paper in case the rest stops are out. You'll also

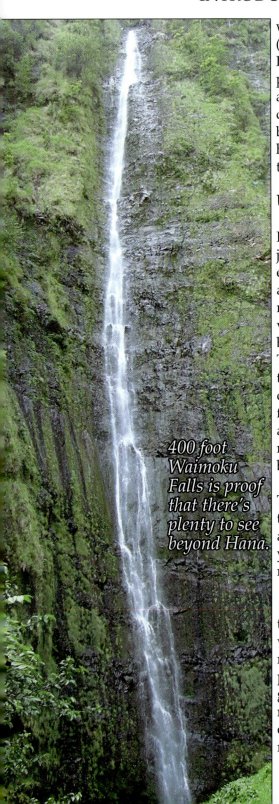

400 foot Waimoku Falls is proof that there's plenty to see beyond Hana.

want some rain gear and sunblock (UV index is normally 12 to 14+ in Hawai'i). Bring bottled water and proper footwear if you plan to hike any of the many stunning trails. A collapsible hiking pole isn't a half-bad idea either; for some of the hikes three or four "legs" are better than two.

USING THIS GUIDE

In this guide we'll embark on a journey covering the majority of east Maui, including both the Hana and Pi'ilani highways. Both are famous for their stunning coastal views, winding curves, one-lane bridges, and never-ending beauty. There are many who will proclaim the Hana Highway to be the best drive in all of Hawai'i, and quite frankly, we're inclined to agree. It's a journey and a drive that is truly magical and should be experienced by all.

This guide has been written for those looking to make the trip along the Hana Highway and beyond. Here are a few things that make our guide unique.

• *Detailed Maps:* Maps…you love them or you hate them, but we've worked hard to make sure our maps are detailed, yet clear and precise. All contain mile markers, general spot locations, cities, landmarks and major roads. We keep our maps simple because some maps are just plain too busy.

• *Place Ratings:* Each spot has a rating (1-5 stars; 5 is best). None of our ratings has been influenced by anyone or anything other than what you will see/experience at each spot. If we liked the place, we'll tell you we liked it, and if we didn't, you're going to know about that too. You'll know what to expect at each spot. We have found that this feature has been very useful for time-strapped travelers. Here are the ratings:

☆☆☆☆☆ - Avoid or Kapu

★☆☆☆☆ - Poor

★★☆☆☆ - So-So

★★★☆☆ - Good

★★★★☆ - Excellent

★★★★★ - Must See

• *Mile Markers:* Mile markers are the best way to describe the location of various spots on Maui. Our guide gives directions based on mile markers around the island so you can locate and view each stop easily. To help distinguish which side of the road spots are on, we don't say "left" or "right" but rather "Mauka" (toward the mountain and center of the island) or "Makai" (toward the ocean). This way, no matter what direction you are travelling, you'll always know which side of the road the spot is on.

In Hawai'i when someone gives you the shaka sign (done by extending the pinkie and thumb while curling the middle fingers) it's a sign of greeting, thanks, or just to say "Hey." Its origins are said to date to the 1930's.

POSSIBLE CLOSURES

In October 2006, there was a significant earthquake off the coast of the Big Island (southeast of Maui). The tremor caused some minor problems in east Maui. Shortly after the quake several portions of the Hana Highway and beyond were closed. Much of this damage was repaired promptly by the county and as of press time, the drive to the 'Ohe'o Gulch was open without any problems. Between Hana and the Gulch, at mile marker 45.5, a temporary bridge still spans the Paihi stream. This bridge has been slated for replacement with a permanent bridge.

The good news is that this bridge will allow you to reach the 'Ohe'o Gulch (Kipahulu area). The bad news is that as you continue beyond the 'Ohe'o Gulch towards Kaupo (half-mile past the 40 mile marker), the road does eventually close (as of press time). The danger of rock slides has prompted the county to close the road to everyone, even residents.

The Pi'ilani Highway (Highway 37) is blocked with concrete pillars just past Charles Lindbergh's grave (page 54) and before Alelele Falls (page 56).

These closures will prohibit vehicles from making the "loop-tour" around east Maui. As a result, you will need to access Highway 37 in Upcountry Maui to view a few of the sites listed at the end of this guide, such as Tedeschi Winery (page 61).

As of press time, the bridge which spans the Manawainui Gulch (page 59-60) is still under repair after the damage it sustained during the earthquake.

It may take up to two years to install the necessary netting to prevent rock slides. More closures along stretches of Highway 37 are expected at unspecified locations as the projects continue.

When driving the Hana Highway we advise checking with the ranger station at the 'Ohe'o Gulch as to road conditions before continuing.

IS THE DRIVE FOR YOU?
Pros & Cons of the Hana Highway

Some of the most frequently asked questions about this journey are, "Is the drive for me?" and "Why all the controversy about the road beyond Hana Town?" Below we'll cover both of these topics.

If you've done any research on the Internet regarding the Hana Highway, then you know there is quite a debate over whether the drive is worth the time and effort. So that brings us to the first question, "Is the Hana Highway right for you and your travel party?" The answer isn't a simple yes or no. Ultimately it really comes down to the type of traveler you are and what your interests include. From a personal standpoint, there is no way we'd ever go to Maui and not drive the highway. But we know others who are just as inclined to tell you to skip it altogether. This divergence in opinion is what causes the great debate.

If you are the type of traveler who wants to see and do as much as you can during your trip (including hiking) and consider yourself an avid outdoors man, then the Hana Highway is definitely something you will want to consider. Just keep in mind that the drive can involve several days of sightseeing (it's hard to do it in a single day) along many miles of winding road (more than 100 miles round-trip). But it's also one of the most beautiful stretches of highway in the entire country. Having visited every state in the Union, we feel we can speak with some authority on that subject. If you are the nature-loving type of traveler, then we highly suggest the Hana Highway for you.

The Hana Highway winds along 52 miles of undeveloped coastline passing over 50 one-lane bridges and 600 turns - and that's just to Hana town.

If you are the type of traveler who is looking to relax, sit back on the beach, hates mosquitoes, and not do a lot of "outdoors stuff," then you might want to rethink the Hana Highway. It is a long drive, and it can be frustrating if your ideal vacation involves a "no-work" attitude. Local residents don't care much for slow-driving visitors on the road and will drive the center line if held up in traffic enough. This frustrates a lot of visitors and really makes the drive a lot less rewarding that it could or should be. As a visitor, use the common courtesy of pulling over from time to time to let residents and/or other travelers by.

With that said, here are a few more things to keep in mind when deciding if you want to make the drive. If you answer "yes" to most of these, then we'd recommend the drive. However, if you feel you are answering "no" to most of these, then you might want to consider spending your time somewhere else.

1.) **Are you, and all the people in your party, comfortable with frequent turns without getting motion sickness?** If not, all the turns might be a rough journey. Since one of us has motion sickness, this was initially a concern. We can gladly say we have not once had anyone ever get sick on this drive. However, we've always been in the front seat of the car together, either driving or observing as a passenger. Passengers in the back seat may have a completely different experience. There are several ways to prevent motion sickness. We prefer the cloth motion sickness wristbands.

2.) **Are you comfortable driving in traffic?** Are you prepared to drive in it at a slow pace if you get started late? Depending on how early you start, you may or may not encounter a lot of traffic. We again stress that 7 a.m. is the very latest to start the journey, and we say that for many reasons, but traffic is definitely one of the larger ones. Your enjoyment, or lack-thereof, can be determined by how you deal with traffic on the highway.

3.) **Do you have the time available for the drive?** There is so much to see on the Hana Highway, in Hana, at the 'Ohe'o Gulch, and beyond to Upcountry Maui that a single day cannot encompass everything. You would honestly be rushing yourself to do this drive with any less than two full days. Whatever you do, never try to make any portion of the drive in the dark. Keep an eye on the time, and if that means skipping places to get started back, do it. The road is not well lit and local traffic can make it more stressful. As we previously recommended, staying a night in Hana would alleviate this problem.

4.) **Are you willing to drive the highway twice?** Many car rental companies technically prohibit the southeast drive, plus the road can often close due to rock slides. That means you may need to turn around and make the drive back. That means 600 turns and 50+ bridges becomes double that number.

5.) **Are you prepared to stop, a lot, to see all the sights?** The Hana Highway is great from a car, but to really appreciate it, you're going to have to stop frequently, get out of the car, and in some cases, walk or hike a bit to see things. For us, this is ideal. But not everyone likes the idea of even light hiking, so keep that in mind when deciding to make the drive or not. The highway is beautiful from a car window, but it definitely cuts down on its "worth" in our book if you aren't likely to step outside the car.

What do they know that I don't? As you make the drive to Hana town you will be continually tempted to pull over and explore locations where other cars are bunched up. We stopped at every pulloff while writing this guide. So if we don't mention it, don't waste your time.

In regards to the second most asked question, "Why the controversy about the road beyond the 'Ohe'o Gulch (Kipahulu)?" First and foremost - and this is for the lawyers - the decision to make the drive is yours alone. If you break down out there, don't say we told you do to it.

Frankly though, don't let the rental companies or alarmists online fool you; the drive beyond the 'Ohe'o Gulch isn't half as bad as they proclaim it is. It's perfectly fine terrain, with just a few rough areas of broken pavement and regularly graded road.

About 30 years ago this was a really bad stretch of road, and at times, due to instability in the cliffs above, it still can be. Hence, it can sometimes close due to rock slides, as it did following the earthquake in 2006.

As noted previously, as of press time, it is still closed for this very reason. If you choose not to make this journey, several of the stops at the end of our guide, in Upcoun-

The scenery beyond the 'Ohe'o Gulch along the Pi'ilani Highway is vastly different from the scenery found just across the island on the Hana Highway.

try Maui, can still be accessed by the fully paved Highway 37.

Hopefully, you're still considering the drive. We don't think you'll be disappointed. No other drive has quite the charm and beauty of the Hana Highway and beyond.

SOME FINAL BASICS
Hazards, weather, and more

Maui's east coast easily could be described as paradise. But even paradise has its hazards, and we'd be foolish not to educate you on at least a few of them. Please make sure you and those who travel with you know about these hazards. Our statements below are rather candid because we want you to know the truth about the place you are visiting. This isn't Disneyland; it is often wild, rough and natural law prevails out here. The more you know, the better prepared you are to avoid the hazards of this beautiful island.

• Wildlife, plants & insects

For the most part you are very safe from all animal and plant life on the Hawaiian Islands. There are no large predators or snakes, and there are few plants that will cause irritation when hiking (no poison oak/ivy, for example). However, other hazards still exist. The main culprit we've come across in the animal world is ac-

tually an insect, the centipede. In Hawai'i these aggressive insects pack quite a punch and getting bit or stung by one is not what you want during your visit to the islands.

Another insect that gets a lot of attention is the cane spider. But it's mostly hype. The brown cane spider is mostly feared due to its size. It is about as big as a can of tuna; that includes its long legs. Typically it will run rather than defend itself, and the bite of a cane spider is rarely dangerous. Nonetheless, we wanted to give it a mention.

There also are scorpions on the drier sides of the island, but they usually stay out of sight. Mosquitoes typically frequent the wetter side of the island, so prepare accordingly.

The edible plants and fruits of Hawai'i also create a hazard. Many visitors believe that they can pop just about anything in their mouths in Hawai'i. Not so. Many plants here are poisonous and no fruit or plant should be eaten unless you absolutely know for sure it is safe. Remember that some plants will have similar looking fruits.

• The sun

A UV index of near 14+ every day speaks for itself. We recommend at least 15+ sunblock in Hawai'i at all times. Don't ruin your visit by trying to get that tropical tan. The tan will be gone within a month of your return home; the memory of the burns will last a lot longer. This is especially important to keep in mind if you're making the drive in a convertible.

• Streams, waterfalls & pools

Our primary message here is short and sweet: Pay attention to the flow of the stream where you are and be aware of the weather inland. Streams and rivers can change flow rates and heights very quickly in the islands. Flash flooding is a regular occurrence in some places. One good rain, even far inland from where you are, can cause a stream to rise substantially. If you're crossing any streams or rock hopping, pay close attention to the weather and the water level.

If you plan to go swimming in a natural stream or pool, or play under a waterfall, make sure you don't swallow any water, and cover any open wounds. Leptospirosis can be found in water contaminated by animal droppings, and you do not want to get mixed up with the likes of this disease. Another note on waterfalls: It's very tempting to get under the many falls along the Hana Highway. Unfortunately, some folks forget about the fact that there are also rocks, logs, and other debris that come over the falls. The larger the falls, the greater the danger.

Kipahulu-area residents also have urged us to point out that swimming at the 'Ohe'o Gulch can be very dangerous at times. The power of the water here is very intense, and the currents near the ocean are deadly. As with all streams, flash flooding can occur with very little warning. Always consult the rangers before swimming, even if you see others in the water.

Rocks also fall over waterfalls. Use caution.

• *Ocean life & the beach*

If you've ever been to the beach then you likely already know about the hazards of the ocean. Rip currents, sharp coral, large waves, surf, and various creatures are just a few. There are select locations you can safely swim in the ocean along this drive, namely Hamoa Beach beyond Hana Town. If you plan to swim anywhere else, especially at any beaches like that found at Wai'anapanapa State Park, make sure to do your homework and become fully educated on the hazards of the ocean before swimming. Pay attention to warning signs.

• *General sightseeing*

There are many locations on Maui that are private property and we have attempted to avoid the use of such properties. If a trail says it's closed, it's closed. If you see a sign that says "Kapu" then it's off-limits. Don't explore places you're not sure about - waterfalls, pools, trails, caves, lava tubes, etc. You likely wouldn't want people exploring your backyard at home, so be mindful and respectful of residents here. Your courtesy will be greatly appreciated.

• *EMI land*

EMI is the East Maui Irrigation company, and they have ditches running most of the way to Hana.

Since they do divert water from various falls and occasionally prevent public access to certain locations, keep that in mind as you explore along the highway. Some waterfalls may be flowing at a lower than usual rate due to EMI diverting water from the stream above the falls.

Their tunnels and ditches feed the cane fields in central Maui. Occasionally they also will block public access to certain locations with "No Trespassing" signs. A few waterfalls along the Hana Highway are completely on or inside EMI areas. We have typically skipped mentioning these spots due to the fact they are on private property and are not legally accessible. The last we heard, EMI was not permitting anyone to hike on its property.

• *Weather conditions*

The best thing about Hawai'i's weather is that it is very localized. You may be driving along the highway and be in a rain storm one minute and in bright sun the next. Maui, like all the other major Hawaiian islands, is affected by the trade winds. These winds blow NE to ENE and are typically more prevalent in the winter months.

These trade winds bring cool air to the islands from the north, often resulting in precipitation along mauka (inland) and windward (facing the trade winds) areas.

The majority of the Hana Highway is along the windward side of Maui. This immediately makes most visitors worry they'll have a soggy trip. Don't. The rain can have its benefits, too. For one, the waterfalls are gorgeous when a storm has just passed. EMI can't catch all that rainwater, so even the sometimes dry and hidden falls burst into view along the highway. In fact, if you make the drive while it's raining, don't be surprised to see a few waterfalls we don't mention at all. Usually they aren't even there.

Since weather can be so unpredictable on Maui, keeping a compact poncho with you during hikes or other outdoor activities is a good idea. As previously noted, the good news about rain is that you're likely only to experience it in short spells. If you do catch the highway on an especially rainy day, rest assured it usually clears up past Nahiku Road (mile marker 25).

• *Crime*

Theft is a reality of driving the Hana Highway. Because many of the stops require you to leave your car and walk to see the sights, anything you leave behind is at risk of being pilfered by miscreants.

Never leave any valuables in your car and always make sure to lock your doors. If you have to leave something, hide it out of sight. Reasonable precautions will ensure a pleasant trip to Hana.

Hana Highway coastline

HANA HIGHWAY
Highway 36 to Highway 360

The official start of the Hana Highway (Highway 36) begins just outside of Kahului, Maui. The maps included throughout this guide should give you a feel for this part of the island and the drive ahead of you. Of course, we always encourage folks to become familiar with these maps ahead of their drive down the highway.

PA'IA TOWN
Mile Marker 6 - Highway 36
★★★☆☆

The journey along the Hana Highway begins at a small town on Maui's north shore named Pa'ia (Pah-ee-ah) town. To get to Pa'ia town from the Kahului Airport, turn onto Highway 36 and follow it to where you enter Pa'ia town beyond mile marker 6.

A little over a hundred years ago Pa'ia was a sugar plantation town. Today it is famous primarily for Ho'okipa Beach Park located just beyond the town. That's our next stop. We highly suggest you fuel up your vehicle here. It's the last gas stop until Hana Town.

It may also be a good place to grab a bite to eat for a picnic lunch later on the drive. Pa'ia has some decent shopping considering its small size, so you might even want to browse through the local shops.

Some would argue that Pa'ia shops are superior to Lahaina stores on the west coast of Maui.

HO'OKIPA BEACH PARK
Mile Marker 8 - Highway 36
★★☆☆☆

As we just mentioned, Ho'okipa Beach Park is located just beyond Pa'ia and Ka'au town makai. You'll pass the steeply graded exit before you pass the entrance, so be looking for the sign marking the spot. There are two very different spots (hangouts) located inside small Ho'okipa Beach Park: one is an overlook that is almost immediately to your right once you turn into the park, and the other is the road that leads down to Ho'okipa Beach itself and then back up to the exit you passed prior to turning into the park at the sign. Ho'okipa Lookout is a nice spot to get a good view over parts of coastal northwest Maui (to your left) and the Pacific Ocean stretching to the north in front of you. It's also a great place to watch surfers and windsurfers catch the waves below you on Ho'okipa Beach.

World-class windsurfing events are held here annually. After you're done at the lookout, your best bet is to get back on Highway 36 and continue your journey. You don't want to waste too much time at this location. Also the beach is a surfer's hangout, so the crowd

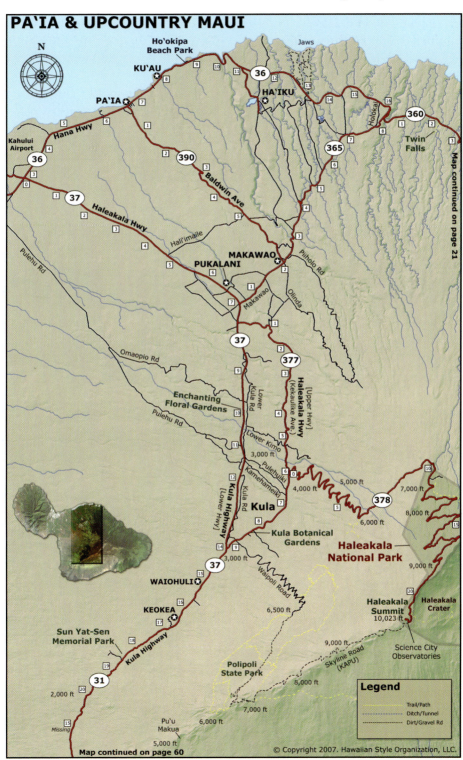

PA'IA & UPCOUNTRY MAUI

N

Ho'okipa
Beach Park

Jaws

KU'AU

9   10

11   36   12

HA'IKU

PA'IA   7

365

5   6

Hana Hwy

1

360

2

Twin
Falls

3

Kahului
Airport   4

36

0

1   37

2

2   390   3

Baldwin Ave

Haleakala Hwy

3

4

Hali'imaile

MAKAWAO

PUKALANI   6

5   1

7   Makawao

Piiholo Rd

2   Olinda

1

Omaopio Rd

37

2

377

Haleakala Hwy
(Kekaulike Ave.)

9

Enchanting
Floral Gardens

10   Lower
Kula Rd

Pulehu Rd

Lower Kimo

11

3,000 ft   Pulehulki

Kamehameiki

Kula Rd

12   7

Kula Highway
[Lower Hwy]

5

8

Kula   4,000 ft   5,000 ft

6,000 ft

7,000 ft

378   8,000 ft

10

15

Kula Botanical
Gardens

**Haleakala
National Park**

14   9

3,000 ft   Waipoli Road

37   15

WAIOHULI

16

6,500 ft

9,000 ft

Haleakala
Summit
10,023 ft

Haleakala
Crater

20

KEOKEA

17

Sun Yat-Sen
Memorial Park

16   Kula Highway

9,000 ft

Skyline Road
(KAPU)

Science City
Observatories

19

31

2,000 ft   20

Polipoli
State Park

8,000 ft

15   Missing

Pu'u
Makua   6,000 ft

7,000 ft

5,000 ft

Map continued on page 60

Map continued on page 21

Legend

Trail/Path
Ditch/Tunnel
Dirt/Gravel Rd

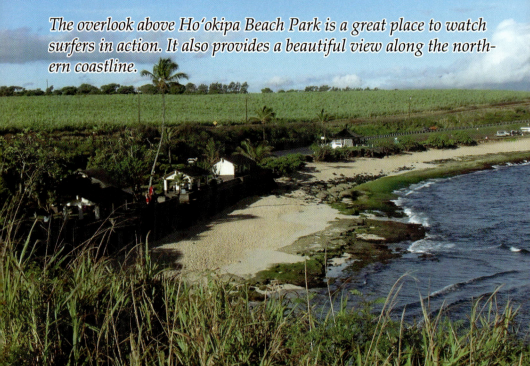

The overlook above Ho'okipa Beach Park is a great place to watch surfers in action. It also provides a beautiful view along the northern coastline.

is not always as full of "aloha" as people in other parts of Maui. We've never had any problems, but there are better beaches on Maui, so why waste your time here?

THE ROAD TO HANA
Highway 360 to Hana Town
Mile Marker 0

As you continue down Highway 36, past mile marker 16, you'll come to the junction of Highway 36 and Highway 360. This is the official start to our journey. Resetting your odometer at the junction will help you keep track of mileage along the drive. The lush vegetation that lines the drive is due in large part to the fact that the Hana Highway skirts the edge of the Ko'olau Forest Reserve (note the highlighted area on the map).

This reserve stretches up to around 4000 feet on the slopes of Haleakala Volcano. Inside this reserve is a tropical paradise of sorts, filled with bamboo, eucalyptus, mango and guava trees. Ko'olau is crisscrossed by a 75-mile network of tunnels and irrigation ditches now overseen by EMI. It leases the land because of the vast amount of rain that this area receives. Near the coast, rainfall averages 60-80 inches a year. Just up the slopes of Haleakala the rainfall jumps to an incredible 200-300 inches a year.

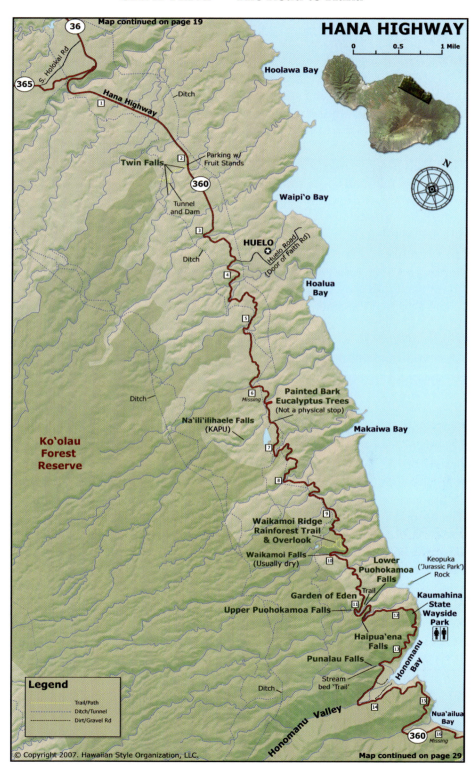

Map continued on page 19

HANA HIGHWAY

0   0.5   1 Mile

36

S. Holokai Rd

365

Hana Highway

Ditch

1

Hoolawa Bay

Twin Falls

2

Parking w/ Fruit Stands

360

Tunnel and Dam

Waipi'o Bay

3

HUELO

Huelo Road (Door of Faith Rd)

Ditch

4

Hoalua Bay

5

6
Missing

Painted Bark Eucalyptus Trees (Not a physical stop)

Na'ili'ilihaele Falls (KAPU)

Makaiwa Bay

Ko'olau Forest Reserve

Ditch

7

8

9

Waikamoi Ridge Rainforest Trail & Overlook

Keopuka ('Jurassic Park') Rock

Waikamoi Falls (Usually dry)

10

Lower Puohokamoa Falls

Trail

Kaumahina State Wayside Park

Garden of Eden

11

Upper Puohokamoa Falls

12

Haipua'ena Falls

13

Punalau Falls

Honomanu Bay

Stream bed 'Trail'

Ditch

14

15
Missing

Nua'ailua Bay

Honomanu Valley

360

16
Missing

Legend

— Trail/Path
- - - Ditch/Tunnel
······ Dirt/Gravel Rd

© Copyright 2007. Hawaiian Style Organization, LLC.

Map continued on page 29

TWIN FALLS & TRAIL
Mile Marker 2 - Highway 360
★★☆☆☆

Just beyond mile marker 2 a bridge crosses the Ho'olawanui stream and here you'll find our first stop, Twin Falls. But first, a word of advice. Twin Falls is a nice stop if you want to view several small falls. Compared to what is ahead of you though, it's really not worth the time to stop here this early in your journey. We have talked with several people who have stopped at this location expecting grand waterfalls they won't find until farther down the road.

If you do decide to stop now (or later) you can pull off and park on the mauka (toward the mountain) side of the road in a small parking lot that is usually accompanied by fruit stands. Walk through the small grassy area to a rock with a map drawn on it. Using this makeshift map you should be able to navigate to the various falls at this location. The round trip takes about an hour.

Beyond Twin Falls, between mile marker 3 and 4, close to Huelo, you'll start to encounter the first really sharp turns in the highway.

NA'ILI'ILI-HAELE [KAPU]
(FOUR WATERFALLS HIKE)
Mile Marker 6 - Highway 360
☆☆☆☆☆

You might read about this spot online or in another guidebook. A half-mile beyond the missing 6 mile marker a trail leads mauka to four different falls. The spot should be considered Kapu, or off-limits. It's located on private EMI property (*see page 16*).

PAINTED BARK
EUCALYPTUS TREES
Mile Marker 6 - Highway 360
★★★☆☆

Between mile markers 6 and 7 you'll find some Painted Bark Eucalyptus trees makai (toward the ocean) in a small grove. These trees have a unique bark that appears to have been hand-painted shades of red, purple and green. This location is not really a stop, as there really isn't much room to pull over. You also can get a glimpse of these trees at Ke'anae Arboretum, which will come later in our journey (*see page 31*).

WAIKAMOI RIDGE TRAIL
(KO'OLAU FOREST RESERVE)
Mile Marker 9 - Highway 360
★★★★★

A little over a half-mile past mile marker 9, keep your eyes open for the parking lot (mauka) to the Waikamoi Ridge Forest Trail and Overlook. It is easy to miss due to the fact it's around a bend in the road. After parking in the often crowded lot, head up to the open area to your left to a small overlook with picnic shelters and the Waikamoi trail head.

Waikamoi forest is one of a kind on Maui. No where else can you stroll through a rainforest and discover the wild side of Maui's Hana Highway.

The Waikamoi Trail is a beautiful, short nature walk through trees, bamboo and ferns with scenic overlooks at various points along the way. There are actually two sections to the trail. One is a short loop that takes about half an hour and ends where it starts (at the picnic area), and the other is a one-way extension from the loop trail. Both trails start at the picnic shelter near the parking area.

When starting the trail(s), we recommend you take the right path at the trailhead. It will take you counterclockwise around the loop and is ultimately an easier hike in that direction. When you get about half way along the loop trail (and at the first lookout bench) you'll notice the extension branching off to the right. This extension is well worth the extra effort because it's always less crowded than the loop trail and will take you farther up the ridge.

At the top of this ridge the trail breaks out of the trees into a grassy clearing with another shelter and picnic site. This overlook offers some remarkable views of the highway and ocean. After you turn to head back, you'll return to the loop trail and take a right onto it. From there the loop trail goes down the ridge to another bench overlook and then along the contour to the beginning point at the trail head.

The trail is usually in good condition, but that can change with just one good rain storm. The worst

An overlook inside the Garden of Eden provides a great view of the Keopuka "Jurassic Park" Rock, used in the opening scenes of the 1993 film.

part of the loop trail (when heading counterclockwise) is the part beyond the extension trail. It goes steeply downhill at times and can be filled with roots. We suspect this will be "fixed" in the future, as volunteer groups have already improved the first half of the loop. There are no facilities at this site, and we do recommend bug spray because mosquitoes like to congregate here.

The Waikamoi Trail is a total of .08 miles if you do the loop trail alone and about 1 1/2 miles if you do the extension. Expect to spend about 30 minutes to an hour here depending on which trails you hike.

WAIKAMOI FALLS
Mile Marker 10 - Highway 360
★★☆☆☆

Between this spot and our next stop you might notice a small waterfall and pool near the bridge mauka on the Waikamoi Stream. Nothing about this falls or pool really warrants a stop unless it has recently rained. Some people don't know this and stop anyway.

A larger falls exists upstream, and after a rainstorm is an incredible sight. If you are driving the road during or after a rainy spell, keep an eye out for the falls which will be partially visible from the highway.

GARDEN OF EDEN BOTANICAL ARBORETUM
Mile Marker 10 - Highway 360
★★★★★

On the mauka side of the highway, a half-mile past mile marker 10, you'll find The Garden of Eden Arboretum & Botanical Garden. We usually don't go into details about private gardens or businesses. But this garden is the exception to the rule. It's one of our favorite stops on the entire drive.

The garden is most popular for its debut in "Jurassic Park." The Keopuka "Jurassic Park" Rock which can be seen from a gorgeous lookout inside the garden was featured in the opening scene of the movie.

The 25-acre site was purchased in 1991 with a vision of restoring the area's natural ecosystem with Hawai'i's native and indigenous species. Along the way the opportunity arose to include exotic plants and trees from the South Pacific region and tropical rain forests throughout the world. Today there are more than 500 botanically labeled plants, including the most extensive collection of Ti plants in Hawai'i. Ti has a long history of usage by the Polynesians in ceremonies and rituals and is still considered one of Hawai'i's most culturally useful plants. You also can get a good look at Upper Puohokamoa Falls (our next stop) from the garden. Several domesticated animals live inside the garden including peafowl, chickens, ducks, geese and even some horses.

If you're lucky you might also run into Bud "The Birdman" Clifton at the exit of the garden. He has a collection of beautiful, well-trained parrots who will gladly pose for a picture with you.

Expect to spend about an hour or two at the garden. Admission is $10 per person as of this printing, but it is well worth it. The garden is open daily from 8 a.m. to 3 p.m. More photos and a map can be found on their web site:

www.MauiGardenOfEden.com

Keopuka Rock

LOWER & UPPER PUOHOKAMOA FALLS
Mile Markers 10-11 - Hwy 360
★★★★☆

Between mile markers 10-11 along the highway there are two impressive waterfalls, Upper & Lower Puohokamoa Falls.

Lower Puohokamoa Falls eludes nearly everyone driving the highway due to its hidden location. This 200-foot waterfall gracefully cascades just below the road as visitors unknowingly speed by. Unfortunately, the best view you can legally get of Lower Puohokamoa Falls is the photo on the opposite page. There used to be a short trail leading from a pull out about .08 of a mile past mile marker 10 which led to the falls, but it now closed to the public. Ownership of the land is in dispute between a private owner and the state of Hawai'i.

Just beyond mile marker 11 there is a bridge and beside it a small parking space (mauka) where a short path leads you to the Upper Puohokamoa Falls and pool. This is the same falls that is visible from the Garden of Eden (*see page 25*).

As of our last visit, the landowner (the Garden of Eden) was restricting access to the falls, so don't be surprised if it's still closed.

Upper Puohokamoa Falls

HAIPUA'ENA FALLS
Mile Marker 11 - Highway 360
★★★☆☆

Located mauka a half-mile past mile marker 11 you'll find Haipua'ena Falls. There is a short trail on the far side of the bridge that can give you an up close and personal view of the falls and pool.

A larger falls upstream feeds Haipua'ena but the hike is usually slippery and risky. On our last visit the lower falls was all that was easily visible. We attempted to get to the upper falls, along with some other folks, and none of us could do it (or were not willing to take the risk up the steep and muddy slope). If you're a die-hard waterfall fan, this stop might be worth the trouble to get to the falls. If not, keep on driving - there are better things ahead.

KAUMAHINA STATE WAYSIDE PARK
Mile Marker 12 - Highway 360
★★★★☆

Just past mile marker 12 you'll find Kaumahina State Wayside Park. This 7.8-acre forested rest stop offers scenic views of the northeast Maui coastline.

One highlight is a spectacular view of the Ke'anae Peninsula and village, an upcoming stop (*see*

Lower Puohokamoa Falls remains one of the hidden gems of the Hana Highway.

page 32). There are also several loop trails that lead uphill from the ocean, giving you a chance to view the many exotic plants.

To make this spot even more attractive, in the spring/summer of 2005 it underwent a major renovation project. Expect to spend 15-30 minutes here, possibly longer if you stop for a picnic lunch or to do a bit of bird watching.

HONOMANU LOOKOUT
Mile Marker 13 - Highway 360
★★★☆☆

Right beyond Kaumahina State Wayside Park you'll find a pullout that gives a good view of Honomanu Bay. From this vantage point you can get another good look at the Ke'anae Peninsula.

PUNALAU VALLEY FALLS
Mile Marker 13 - Highway 360
★★★☆☆

If you've been looking for a waterfall you can enjoy all to yourself, you might be in luck at this next spot. Punalau Falls' waters tranquilly slide down the steep slope at the end of the small Punalau Valley. To access the falls, pull off on the far side of the bridge around a quarter-mile past mile marker 13.

If you head up the Punalau streambed while doing some serious rock skipping, at around 800 or so feet up the valley (it'll feel like longer than that) you should reach the falls. If you're lucky, you'll have the falls all to yourself. The walk up the streambed on the rocks can take anywhere from 10-25 minutes one way. Use caution heading up the streambed, and avoid the spot if the stream is flowing too heavily.

HONOMANU BAY ACCESS ROADS
Mile Marker 13-14 - Highway 360
★★☆☆☆

Between mile markers 13 and 14 you will have a chance to visit Honomanu Bay, which you just saw from above at mile marker 13. There are two roads that lead to the beach. The first is about a half-mile beyond the 13 mile marker - but this dirt road brings you out on the wrong side of the beach (the stream will cut you off from the remainder of the shoreline). The other access road is available just beyond the 14 mile marker. This route is much muddier, steeper, and a 4x4 may be required at times, so you might have to walk to the beach instead. Taking your car off-road is a violation of your rental agreement anyway.

Like many beaches in Hawai'i, the amount of sand can vary from the winter to summer. In the winter months the beach can be mostly small rocks and boulders. In the summer the changing tides will cause the sand to return. The beach is frequented by surfers, especially in the winter months. Swimming is ill-advised due to rough surf. In our opinion, the best way to view this bay is from above (at mile marker 13 or one of the upcoming lookouts).

VARIOUS LOOKOUTS
Mile Marker 14 - Highway 360
★★★★★

Between mile markers 14 and 16 there are several dirt and/or broken pavement pullouts on the makai side of the road that provide really beautiful lookouts. Most are as good as any other, but the two we've noted next are our favorites and are worth a quick stop.

THE HANA HIGHWAY

Map continued on page 21

Punalau Falls
Honomanu Bay
Nua'ailua Bay
KE'ANAE
360 Missing
Trail
Ke'anae Arboretum
Ching's Pond
Pauwalu Pt
Spring
← Ko'olau Gap
(open to Haleakala Crater)
Honomanu Valley
Waiokilo Falls
Wailua Valley State Wayside
WAILUA
Ke'anae Valley
Ditch
Lower Waikani Falls
Visible from Wailua
Upper Waikani Falls
(aka '3 Bears Falls')
Lower Wailuaiki Falls
Ko'olau Forest Reserve
Waiohue Bay
Missing
Nahiku Landing
Pua'a Ka'a Falls
(aka 'Waiohue Falls')
Pua'a Ka'a State Park
Upper Hanawi Falls
Hana Highway
Ditch
Nahiku Road (Scenic)
Makapipi Falls
360

0   0.5   1 Mile

N

Map continued on page 37

Legend
.... Trail/Path
--------- Ditch/Tunnel
········· Dirt/Gravel Rd

The lookouts at mile marker 14 offer incredible 180-degree views.

Makai, around mile marker 14, there is a pullout that overlooks the Hana Highway and Honomanu Bay back to your left (*photo on page 6*). This is a perfect location to take a picture of the winding highway along with Honomanu Bay.

Down the road a bit farther is another pullout, this time on a steep embankment with trees on top. This is the last place you can see such an expansive view of the highway as it twists and turns around the shore heading for Hana Town (*see photograph above*).

What makes it our favorite, however, is that while the Hana Highway is impressive on the left, the view of Ke'anae Peninsula on the right is perfect from this vantage point.

NUA'AILUA BAY LOOKOUT
Mile Marker 16 - Highway 360
★★★☆☆

From mile marker 16 (which is missing a physical marker) you can look back and get an excellent view of steep and rugged Nua'ailua Bay to your left. This vantage point is quite different from the previous lookout - notice the cliff-like walls channeling the waves into this bay versus the gently sloping shoreline of Honomanu.

KE'ANAE ARBORETUM
Mile Marker 16 - Highway 360
★★★★☆

A half-mile beyond mile marker 16 you'll see a sign on the mauka side of the road marking the entrance to Ke'anae Arboretum. The arboretum is large, with a paved parking lot makai after the sign. Because of the sloped curve in the road, be careful crossing the street from the parking area to the arboretum.

The Ke'anae Arboretum lies alongside the Pi'ina'au Stream on leveled terraces built hundreds of years ago for growing taro, a mainstay of their diet. A 0.6-mile paved walkway takes visitors through timber, fruit and ornamental trees from tropical regions around the world, many of which are marked with nameplates. Inside the arboretum you can find some 150 varieties of tropical plants (including taro). This is a great location to see some indigenous flowers and the painted bark eucalyptus trees.

An upper section of the arboretum features plants cultivated by the Hawaiians for food and other uses. This arboretum appears to have undergone major renovations which included an expansion on the previous path that now leads into beautiful small taro fields not previously located in the arboretum.

There are no facilities or amenities at this stop. Expect to spend 30 minutes to an hour here.

The taro fields of Ke'anae Arboretum allow you to view the staple crop of the ancient Hawaiian people up close.

Pauwalu Point as seen from the coast. Moku mana offshore. Ke'anae Peninsula (far right) and Ko'olau Gap (rear left).

KE'ANAE PENINSULA
Mile Marker 16 - Highway 360
★★★★☆

Immediately after leaving Ke'anae Arboretum look for and turn onto the road that splits off the highway makai with a sign labeled "Ke'anae Peninsula."

The peninsula is surrounded by dark, jagged lava that serves as a vivid reminder of the ancient flows from Haleakala that formed this place. Hala trees along the shore are the only plant that can get a grip on this gnarled coastline. Down the road about 0.75 of a mile there is a large dirt parking lot across from the church and ball field.

The views along the coastline here are incredible. The huge waves and the surf around the peninsula should be more than enough reason to keep out of the water. Off to your right you will see Pauwalu Point in the distance. Just offshore is Moku Mana island, a seabird sanctuary *(visible in photo above)*.

A pristine stream runs along the back cliff of the peninsula, but the accompanying pools and falls border private property and should be avoided. Further up the stream is Ching's Pond, our next stop.

Life here is tranquil, but this has not always been the case. On April 1, 1946, life on the peninsula changed forever when a devastating tsunami hit this side of the island. It completely washed over the peninsula, killing 20 children and 4 teachers. The only building that survived was 'Ihi'ihio Iehowa o na Kaua Church (Ke'anae Congregational Church). The church is still standing in the town today, a somber reminder of what has happened here in the past, and likely will again in the future.

CHING'S POND
(SAPPHIRE POOLS)
Mile Marker 16 - Highway 360
★★★☆☆

About 0.8 mile past mile marker 16, a bridge crosses Palauhulu stream (the same stream that empties into the ocean at Ke'anae Peninsula below). Beneath the bridge is a series of pristine (sapphire) pools that you won't be able to view from the road.

Access is via two trails on the makai side of the bridge before you cross it. The trail immediately next to the bridge is very steep, very difficult, and should be avoided. A bit farther to the left of the bridge, about 50 feet over is a large tree. There is a trail here too, and it's significantly easier to get down to the pools this way.

A few of the pools are mauka of the bridge in a constricted gorge that flushes the water through at a very quick rate. Use caution swimming here. A small water chute empties into a lower pool makai of the bridge. Never dive into this or any other pool at this stop. The pools can get crowded occasionally and local residents also tend to stop here frequently, especially on weekends.

KE'ANAE LOOKOUT
Mile Marker 17 - Highway 360
★★★☆☆

Around mile marker 17 there is an easy-to-miss pulloff to the makai side of the road (look for the tsunami warning speaker). From this location you can get a really nice view overlooking the Ke'anae Peninsula. The little square fields/patches are actually taro ponds.

WAILUA TOWN & LOWER WAIKANI FALLS
Mile Marker 18 - Highway 360
★★☆☆☆

Just makai beyond mile marker 18 is the small road leading down to Wailua Town. While there isn't much for visitors to do or see in the town itself, the spot is worth a mention due to the fact it's the only place you can catch a glimpse of Lower Waikani Falls. This falls is on the Wailuanui stream and is one of the largest falls under the highway. From the town road, you should be able to get a partial view of the falls by looking

Ke'anae Valley (Ko'olau Gap) as seen from Wailua Wayside Park

inland, back up the mountain. It's a nice side-trip if you have the time. If not, you can get a more intimate view of another falls on the same stream in a few minutes. Upper Waikani Falls is just ahead.

WAILUA VALLEY STATE WAYSIDE PARK
Mile Marker 18 - Highway 360
★★★☆☆

A little over a half-mile past mile marker 18, mauka, you'll come to Wailua Valley State Wayside Park. Most visitors breeze right by and never even realize it's there. The park provides perspectives of the Ke'anae Valley (a lower portion of the Ko'olau Gap in Haleakala's crater) and an overlook of Wailua Village. It's not a major attraction, but it's worth a stop for some great scenic views. After parking, take the stairs up to the lookout on your right. If you're interested, a paved overlook another quarter-mile down the highway provides an even better look at Wailua town.

UPPER WAIKANI FALLS (THREE-BEARS FALLS)
Mile Marker 19 - Highway 360
★★★★★

Mauka a half-mile beyond mile marker 19 you'll find beautiful Upper Waikani (Three-Bears Falls). This is one of the most visited waterfalls in the area. You can get

Waikani Falls is proof that sometimes less (waterflow) is more.

a great view of this triple-spouted beauty from the side of the road. If you'd like to get a bit closer, there is a path at the Hana end of the bridge which leads you right to the falls. The trail is accessible from mauka and makai sides of the bridge, but makai is easier. Simply climb down and under the bridge and follow the jungle-like path towards the falls and then rock-skip a few feet up to the best vantage point. This is a really great way to view the falls up close and personal. The photo on the previous page may make the falls look fairly small, but it's actually 70 feet tall!

The falls can change in (flow) size dramatically depending on rainfall. In the winter months the falls can be huge, unapproachable, and even unattractive, whereas in the spring and summer it can ideally be much smaller (*as seen on the previous page*).

WAILUAIKI FALLS
Mile Marker 21 - Highway 360
★★☆☆☆

Near the 21 mile marker you'll cross over Wailuaiki Stream Bridge. If you can find a place to park (usually just beyond the bridge), pull over and take a look at the 50-foot waterfall cascading just under the bridge. This stream and waterfall can dry up if it hasn't rained lately, as the East Maui Irrigation (EMI) company diverts a

lot of the water upstream. Speaking of upstream, a hunters road/trail starts mauka just up the road from the bridge and goes to a variety of other waterfalls upstream that are almost always flowing, but this trail is on EMI land. See page 16 for more information about hiking in restricted EMI areas.

PUA'A KA'A STATE WAYSIDE PARK
Mile Marker 22 - Highway 360
★★★☆☆

Farther down the highway, around a half-mile past mile marker 22, you'll find Pua'a Ka'a State Wayside Park (that's always fun to say). Here you'll find a paved trail to several small falls and a picnic area. A larger falls can also be accessed upstream via a dirt trail. This trail crosses EMI land and cannot be taken without permission. If you decide to go, use caution crossing the viaduct and be prepared for mud.

Mongooses (yes that's plural) also hang out at the park. You may already have seen them streaking across the road. Some bright soul imported them to kill the rats that the sailors brought here on their boats. Well, they killed the ground rats and most of the ground birds, but left the tree rats. The mongoose is now found on every island except Kaua'i. The little creatures run around this area gathering food left over from picnics. You also are likely

Nahiku Road is the type of place you slow down…Hawaiian style.

to see the wild jungle foul (chickens) that frequent the area (that is, if the mongooses haven't gotten to them yet).

The large paved parking lot at this stop will be makai. Restrooms are available here as well.

UPPER HANAWI FALLS
Mile Marker 24 - Hwy 360
★★★☆☆

Our next official stop is right after mile marker 24. Here you'll find Upper Hanawi Falls. This is one of many falls that the Hanawi Stream creates in its nine-mile path to the ocean. Because the stream is spring-fed, many of the falls can even be seen during the drier summer months. A large rain shower can have a great effect on the flow of Hanawi Falls. The safest way to view the falls is from the bridge.

MAKAPIPI FALLS
Mile Marker 25 - Highway 360
★★★☆☆

As you cross the bridge over Makapipi stream near mile marker 25 be sure to stop to check out the falls under the bridge. Here you'll find Makapipi Falls, one of the most interesting falls on the Hana Highway. The Makapipi Stream flows within the lava streambed into a pristine blue pool. The Hana Highway crosses directly over the

HANA HIGHWAY

0   0.5   1 Mile

Helele'ike'oha
(Blue Angel Falls & Pool)
(KAPU)

Private Land

Pi'ilanihale Heiau

Kahanu Garden

Map continued on page 29

360

Hana Highway

'Ula'ino Rd

Maia   Uwala

Alalele

Hana Airport

Kalo

Freshwater Caves

Honokalani

Pa'iloa Bay

Honokalani Black Sand Beach

Wai'anapanapa Wayside Park

Coastal Trail

360

Waikoloa

HANA TOWN

Uakea

Waikoloa

Hana Bay

Kauiki

NoeNoe

Alau

Keanini

Keawa

Hana Highway

Uakea

Hauoli

Hana Cultural Center

Pu'u Ki'i Lighthouse

Hana Beach Park

Pier

Keawa

Hana Community Center

Ka'uiki Head

Red Pocket Beach

Paul Fagan Memorial Cross

Hana Store

Mill Place

Trail

Hasegawa General Store

Kaihalulu Beach
(Red Sand Beach)

N

34

Uakea

Kainalimu Bay

Hana Bay

Ka'uiki Head

Kaihalulu Beach
(Red Sand Beach)

31

Ka Iwi o Pele
(The Bones of Pele)

Sea Arch

Koki Beach

'Alau Island

Fish Ponds

South Hana Hwy

Haneo'o Road

Hamoa Beach

N

Map continued on page 46

Legend

———— Trail/Path
·········· Ditch/Tunnel
– – – – Dirt/Gravel Rd

stream allowing folks a view of the falls over the bridge railing. The flow of the falls is dependent on rainfall, but if flowing is very intriguing to witness.

To access this spot, park just beyond the bridge where there is a small pull off and walk back onto the bridge to look down on the makai side of the road.

NAHIKU ROAD & LANDING
Mile Marker 25 - Highway 360
★★★★★

Just a few yards past mile marker 25, just around the bend from the previous stop, you should see a steep downhill turnoff for Nahiku Road makai. The road is lush and surrounded by a jungle setting - even the trees have plants growing on them. With 300 inches of rain per year, no wonder Nahiku is a paradise for all things green. The road is lined with rubber trees, remnants from a plantation that went defunct nearly 100 years ago. You'll barely noticed passing Nahiku village except for the occasional house and a variety of abandoned vehicles, now property of the jungle around them.

At the end of the road (about 2.5 miles down) you'll come to the gorgeous scenic bay at Opuhano Point. Looking to your left over Honolu-

Opuhano Point & Honolulunui Bay at Nahiku Landing

lunui Bay, the coastal views are some of the very best on the entire road to Hana. You can see all the way back to Wailua.

As you try to absorb all of the scenery, take a moment to listen, too. Off to the right, near the small ledge where the waves pound the shore, you'll find thousands of pebbles being rolled back and forth in the surf. The harmonic sound of the rolling rocks is quite unique, mother nature's own rock tumbler in action.

From this point forward the "enclosed" feel of the highway starts to open up a bit as you get closer to Hana Town. You'll also start to pass more houses and developed areas. Here's a quick synopsis of what you'll see between Nahiku Landing and our next stop at Ula'ino Road. Just beyond mile marker 26 you'll pass some houses, garden and floral stands, and eventually you'll pass by some run-down looking areas right beyond mile marker 27. The heavy rain makes everything look 10 to 20 years older than it really is here.

You'll also start to get some pretty good views of Haleakala's north east face. Closer to mile marker 30 the road begins to open up to the fantastic scenery of the Pacific Ocean. At mile marker 31 you'll officially be welcomed to Hana Town with a sign mauka side, and shortly thereafter you'll see the turnoff for the small Hana airport.

ULA'INO ROAD
KAHANU GARDEN, PI'ILANI HEIAU, KA'ELEKU CAVERNS, & HELELE'IKE'OHA [KAPU]
Mile Marker 31 - Highway 360
★★★☆☆

Our next stops, located on Ula'ino Road, are about a half-mile beyond mile marker 31 makai. You have a variety of choices down this road. You can go spelunking at Ka'eleku Caverns, stroll along the coast in beautiful Kahanu Garden, or visit Hawai'i's oldest and largest place of worship, Pi'ilanihale Heiau.

Not quite a half-mile down the road, the large yellow sign marking Ka'eleku Caverns is hard to miss. Tours are self-guided and offer visitors the chance to explore a Hana lava tube. The caverns are open six days a week from 10:30 a.m. to 3:30 p.m. As of this printing the admission cost was $11.95 per person.

Just after a mile, the road gives way to broken pavement and the first stream ford. Beyond the ford, to the right, you'll find the entrance to Kahanu Garden, an extension of the National Tropical Botanical Garden. If the ford has water flowing through it above the pole-markers, turn around and do not try and cross the stream.

The 122-acre garden is home to a variety of rare native Hawaiian plants and several trees introduced by the Polynesians. The garden also has one of the largest known collections of breadfruit trees. A mile long trail meanders through the garden, allowing visitors to be their own tour guide. Beyond the forest edge you'll find the impressive and colossal Pi'ilanihale Heiau.

The heiau was constructed completely out of lava rock in the 14th century during the reign of the Pi'ilani Dynasty. The stone platform is the size of two football fields. Visitors are not allowed on the heiau, so you'll have to view it from afar. The coastal views here are beautiful.

As of this printing, the garden is open Monday - Friday, 10 a.m. - 2 p.m. Admission is $10 for adults and free for children. It closes without notice, so don't be surprised if you find "Closed" signs.

Farther down at the end of Ula'ino Road (another 1.5 miles down from Kahanu Garden) there is a much-talked-about falls and pools you might know as "Blue Pool," "Blue Angel Falls," or another name. Locally it's known as Helele'ike'oha Falls. At the end of the road you'll be bombarded with "Parking" signs followed by "No Trespassing" signs. What gives?

The beach is public access, but getting to it is not. This spot and the surrounding residents are the victims of too much publicity. A few thousand visitors a day now head down muddy Ula'ino Road to view the falls and pool, and to do so, they must ALL cross private property. This has caused quite a few problems in the area.   But who can blame the landowners for being upset? If you had a thousand people a day tromping through your backyard, it'd probably upset you too. Our opinion is that visitors should show some Aloha and skip this spot, better things are ahead.

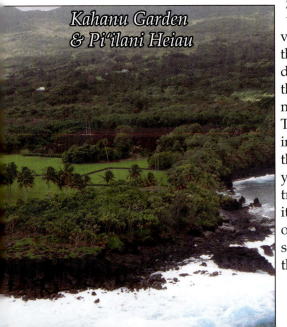

Kahanu Garden & Pi'ilani Heiau

Wai'anapanapa's black sand beach is one of the major attractions of the drive.

WAI'ANAPANAPA STATE WAYSIDE PARK
Mile Marker 32 - Highway 360
★★★★★

Getting ever closer to Hana Town, we have one last major stop, at mile marker 32. On the makai side of the highway you should see a gravel road leading down to Wai'anapanapa State Wayside Park. There also should be a road sign informing you of the location. Head down the road and look for the main parking area (to the left), near the cabins. From here a trail will lead you down to Honokalani black sand beach, located in Pa'iloa Bay. Swimming is dangerous and should be avoided here. The beach is open to the ocean with no outside reef to break the force of the waves and current. You will see many warning signs because of this. Once you're on the beach, you might be interested in exploring the cave opening off to your right. Though narrow at the entrance, it widens inside and takes you to an open view of the ocean at the other end.

The black sand beach isn't the only attraction at Wai'anapanapa, though. Wai'anapanapa (Why-Ah-naa-paa-naa-paa) also features sculpted lava rocks, wind twisted foliage, a sea arch, lava caves and tubes, and even a "blow hole" in the lava rocks near the shoreline. The area around the park is also very interesting to hike through. There are a few "wet" caves and

Hana Town & Bay

HANA TOWN & BAY
Mile Markers 33 to 34
End of Hwy 360
★★★☆☆

After leaving Wai'anapanapa State Park you'll turn left back onto the highway and pass the Hana Town schools just before entering Hana Town itself. You will come to a fork in the road at the entrance of the town, the left fork takes you down to Hana Bay in about a mile, and the right fork takes you into "downtown" Hana with its stores, shops, and restaurants (map on page 37). The right fork is also the direct route to Highway 31 and all the adventures that lie beyond Hana Town.

Hana is a 4,500-acre area previously owned by the Unna Brothers who, in the 1800's, raised sugar cane. In 1935, the area was bought by Paul Fagan, who began raising cattle in the area. Today the Hana area is owned by a group of local and mainland investors.

Hana is a quaint town that offers Maui visitors a place to relax away from the mainstream lives they've almost all come to escape. Hana is certainly the place to go to get away from it all. You can grab a bite to eat at one of the three restaurants in town, go shopping in one of the small stores, and even "talk story" (chat) with some of the local folks. We always like to joke with them about the cars parked on the Hana Highway and the fact that

lava tubes with fresh water running through them. They can be reached by walking beyond the beach access point; to the left, look for the trail signs to the caves. The overgrown path will lead you down to a series of pools and caves before looping back the way it came.

More hiking is available to the southeast, where you could technically hike all the way to Hana Town. A mile down this trail is Ohala Heiau. Keep an eye out for the blowhole as you hike to the heiau.

The large variety of sea birds here may be of interest to bird watching enthusiasts as well. Restrooms and picnic tables are available.

they have been there for about two decades now. "Oh they're part of the scenery of the highway now, just too expensive to tow them out," they say with a smile. And in Hana Town, a smile is about as genuine a smile as you'll ever find.

If you have some time to spare, stop by the Hana Cultural Center on Ke'anini Street to view its collection of Hawaiian art and artifacts. Admission is free.

While you're in Hana take a moment to stop by Hana Bay where you'll find a large black sand beach. The black sand was formed as lava eroded slowly over time, eventually washing up around the bay. Swimming is usually pretty good, but be sure to check with a local resident before jumping in.

The Hana pier is located on the right side of the bay and offers a unique view of Hana Town if you have a chance to walk out on it. The large hill at the far right end of the bay is Ka'uiki Hill. If you walk to the end of the road where the pier begins, you should be able to find a trail heading up and around the hill. If you follow it a while you can get some nice views of the Hana coastline, Hana Town, and even visit a small red sand pocket beach about 200 yards into the hike. Sand can vary at the beach throughout the year, so don't expect much. The best treat along this hike is the view of Hana Town with Haleakala in the background.

KAIHALULU
(RED SAND BEACH)
In Hana Town - Off Ua'kea Road
★★★☆☆

A more popular beach is just on the other side of Ka'uiki hill. This beach is known as Kaihalulu (Red Sand) beach. The beach gets its red sand from lava cinders off Ka'uiki. The quickest way to access this beach is to take Ua'kea road past Hana Bay to where it dead ends at Hauoli Road. Make sure you park your car in the right direction (depending on which side of the road you're on - Hana police will ticket you otherwise).

The 'Red Sand Beach' can be seen here on the backside of Ka'uiki Hill. Hana town is around the hill to the right.

Koki Beach is uncrowded and ready for sunbathers. 'Alau Island (upper left)

The trail to the beach begins across from the Sea Ranch Cottages. It can be tricky in places and is fairly steep. At the bottom of the trail you'll find an interesting sign that both informs you of "No Trespassing" and then "Use At Your Own Risk"- interesting. We've talked with several local residents and none of them raised any concern about visitors frequenting the beach. We highly advise against swimming or snorkeling here, as the water can be treacherous.

BEYOND HANA TOWN
Highway 31 to 'Ohe'o Gulch

Once you've seen beautiful Hana, you'll likely be eager to begin your journey beyond. At the far edge of Hana Town after taking the right fork you'll almost unknowingly leave Highway 360 (Hana Highway) and begin on Highway 31 (South Hana Highway), heading towards Highway 37 (Haleakala Highway). Our maps will help clarify these routes.

It is important to note that the mile markers leading away from Hana Town are COUNTING DOWN, not up. This is opposite what you experienced coming into Hana Town.

On Highway 31 you should also be aware that the mile markers count down until mile marker 15, then they jump back to 20 and go down again. We're not sure about the logic in that, but none-the-less, keep that in mind.

KOKI BEACH & 'ALAU ISLAND
Haneo'o Road off Highway 31
★★★☆☆

On Highway 31, more than a half mile past mile marker 51 beyond Hana Town, you'll come to a road on the makai side of the highway named Haneo'o Road. The hill to your left is an eroding cinder cone known as Ka Iwi o Pele (the bones of Pele).

Driving down Haneo'o Road, the rugged cliffs give way to a beautiful coastal view. As you continue down towards the shore you'll notice 'Alau Island offshore. From this vantage point it looks like a small island with a few trees perched on top.

About 100 yards down the road as it starts to level off, you'll notice a pulloff to the left. This is the Koki Beach overlook. From here you also can get an excellent view of 'Alau Island with its swaying palms directly offshore. Look to your left and you'll also be able to view a sea arch off in the distance on the rocky coast. Use caution swimming.

Between Koki Beach and our next stop, Hamoa Beach, look for the ancient Haneo'o fishponds.

This photograph by Forest Starr of the USGS helps put the true size of 'Alau island into perspective. Koki Beach can be seen to the right in the background.

Map continued on page 37

Koki Beach

50

Fishponds

Haneo'o Road

31

Hamoa Beach

49

48   Private Land

Waioka Pond (Venus Pool) (KAPU)

South Hana Hwy

Keawa Bay

47

Waiho'i Valley

Ala'alaula Falls

46

Waihiumalu Falls (Visible from Highway)

Kanahauli'i Falls

Paihi Falls

Kekuapo'owai Falls

Kauakio Bay

45

Wailua Falls

Wailua Cove

Kipahulu Gap

44

*Note: Beyond the 'Ohe'o Gulch the Pi'ilani Highway may close unexpectedly due to danger of rock slides. Check all road conditions at the 'Ohe'o Gulch Visitor Center before continuing beyond that point.

Hahalawe Falls

Wai'a'ama Bay

Pua'a-lu'u Falls

43

Waimoku Falls

Haleakala National Park (Kipahulu Area)

Bamboo Forest

Makahiku Falls

42

'Ohe'o Gulch (aka 7 Sacred Pools)

Visitor Center

Kuloa Point

Trails

Pipiwai Stream Trail (4 Miles RT)

Kukui Bay

N

41

Lindbergh's Grave

Pi'ilani Hwy

Alelele Falls

40   31

Ma'ulili Bay

Legend

Trail/Path
Ditch/Tunnel
Dirt/Gravel Rd

39   'Trail'

Lekekea Bay

Kukui'ula Falls

Parking

0   0.5   1 Mile

38

Narrow Road (Approx. 2 Miles)

Map continued on page 57

SOUTH HANA HIGHWAY

Hamoa Beach is one of our favorite beaches in Hawai'i. Can you blame us?

HAMOA BEACH
Haneo'o Road off Highway 31
★★★★★

Heading farther down the road beyond Koki Beach you'll discover one of the most beautiful beaches in all of Hawai'i - the world famous Hamoa Beach.

After parking in the lot at the beach, proceed down the stairs to the shoreline. The surrounding grounds are nearly as captivating as the beach itself. Hamoa is about 1,000 feet long and 100 feet wide with sea cliffs surrounding it. Lush vegetation cradles the beach in stunning beauty.

Off shore there is decent snorkeling and scuba diving, good swimming, and just as in ancient times, excellent body surfing, too (mostly in the winter). If you can wrestle a kayak down to the beach, launching is relatively easy when the surf is down. Hamoa is unprotected by fringing reefs, so big surf hits the beach unimpeded in the winter months.

The beach is surrounded by private property owned by the Hotel Hana Maui. Most of the facilities are for the guests of the resort, but the Hotel Hana Maui allows the use of some of the facilities. Restrooms, showers and picnic tables are available.

After leaving the beach you'll continue on down Haneo'o Road, passing several small communities and houses. There really isn't much to see beyond Hamoa Beach, so we recommend you just drive straight back to the highway. When you reach Highway 31 again you'll want to turn left to continue your journey. You will be getting on right before mile marker 49 (remember, the mile markers are now counting down).

Wailua Falls (heavier flow)

WAIOKA POND [KAPU] (VENUS POOL)
Mile Marker 48 - Highway 31
☆☆☆☆☆

Venus Pool, also known locally as Waioka Pond, isn't the well kept secret it once was, and the popularity of the spot has caused some tension over access to it. The path just across the fence may tempt you. But several residents have informed us that there is no safe or legal way (without trespassing) to reach the pool. Additionally, many visitors have been ticketed at this location by police. It begs the question, is this all really worth it? In our opinion, no! There is just too

much controversy surrounding this spot and it's too difficult to access, so we recommend you skip it and continue to 'Ohe'o instead. If you still choose to swim here, avoid the end of the pool where the stream enters the ocean; there is a bad undertow.

ALA'ALAULA FALLS
Mile Marker 46 - Highway 31
★★☆☆☆

Just beyond the 46 mile marker, you will pass over Ala'alaulua Bridge. Next to the bridge, mauka, is a small waterfall. It's nothing special, and better falls are right around the corner.

PAIHI FALLS
Mile Marker 46 - Highway 31
★★★☆☆

Just before mile marker 45 you'll pass over Paihi stream. As of press time, this stream is spanned by a temporary bridge (see page 9). Here you'll also find a small roadside waterfall called Paihi Falls that drops about 50 feet just beside the road.

WAILUA STREAM
Mile Marker 45 - Highway 31

Around mile marker 45 you'll cross over Wailua stream. Yet you won't find Wailua Falls here. The falls is actually our next stop, on Honolewa Stream (oddly enough). So why the mention of the stream? Upstream exist two beautiful falls, Kanahuali'i Falls and Waihiumalu Falls. Unfortunately you

Wailua Falls (lighter flow)

can't visit either, but you can view one of them from the highway. Not to get ahead of ourselves, but shortly after you pass Wailua Falls, at the top of a hill, glance behind you up on the cliff. You should be able to catch a glimpse of the upper falls on the stream, Waihiumalu Falls (400 ft).

WAILUA FALLS
Mile Marker 45 - Highway 31
★★★★★

Just beyond mile marker 45 you'll reach one of the most gorgeous falls in all of Hawai'i, Wailua Falls. You will cross a bridge where its stream waters pass under the road. As noted, this falls is on Honolewa Stream and not Wailua stream. There is a parking lot immediately off to the makai side after you pass the falls. Wailua Falls gracefully cascades 80 feet through a lush setting in the surrounding vegetation just feet from the road.

There is a short path to the base of the falls, but it can be tricky so use caution. The water flow varies but is usually pretty throughout the year. Upstream exists Kekuapo'owai Falls, but unfortunately it is only visible by helicopter.

Pua'a Lu'u Falls and another small waterfall (Hahalawe Falls) are both located a little farther down the road from Wailua Falls. There's a pullout on the side of the road past the bridge at Pua'a Lu'u Falls, and the short path (look for the giant tree) downstream to the falls is also worth a brief stop.

The Pools of 'Ohe'o are the highlight of the drive beyond Hana Town.

'OHE'O GULCH & KIPAHULU AREA
Mile Marker 42 - Highway 31
End of the Hana Highway
★★★★★

About 15 minutes past Hana, near mile marker 42, is the 'Ohe'o Gulch at the east end of Haleakala National Park. In 1969, the land where the 'Ohe'o Gulch is situated (formally known as Kipahulu coastal area) was donated to the Haleakala National Park system so the pools would forever be open to the public.

The 'Ohe'o Gulch today is known by many names. Some call it the

Kipahulu Area, while others call it the location of the Seven Sacred Pools. However, there are far more than just seven pools, so the name is quite inaccurate. It originates from a 1940's publicity campaign. There are actually dozens of pools and a multitude of waterfalls that flow through the 'Ohe'o Gulch into the nearby ocean. This is one of the best spots to visit on Maui and is well worth a few hours of your time.

After crossing the bridge over the stream, the parking lot is located makai. The fee for visiting the park is only $10 per vehicle and is valid for this part of Haleakala National Park, as well as the road that leads to the summit of Haleakala (see page 64).

Starting some two miles inland, the Palikea and Pipiwai Streams are the source of water for all of the falls in this area. These streams join inland to form a string of pools along the 'Ohe'o Gulch. The easiest to reach and the nicest pools are located near the shoreline right beyond the Park Ranger's building.

KULOA POINT TRAIL
Mile Marker 42 at 'Ohe'o Gulch
★★★★★

A half-mile easy loop trail leads from the Kipahulu Visitor Center down to the ocean at Kuloa Point past historic walls and pre-contact Hawaiian habitation sites. The trail passes a grove of hala trees on the way to beautiful views of the ocean and several large pools.

Swimming is permitted when conditions allow it. Never jump into the water from the cliffs above. Also, the ocean currents at Kuloa Point are very strong and sharks and high surf are constant dangers. Do not go into the ocean here; stay in the pools above if you swim.

KAHAKAI TRAIL
Mile Marker 42 at 'Ohe'o Gulch
★★★☆☆

The Kahakai Trail stretches a quarter-mile between Kuloa Point and the Kipahulu campground. Shoreline views along the ocean are beautiful, but be mindful of your step. Of the three trails in the area, this is the one to skip, but given that it's so short you might as well enjoy it while here.

PIPIWAI TRAIL
Mile Marker 42 at 'Ohe'o Gulch
★★★★★

The Pipiwai Trail is a moderately strenuous 4-mile round-trip trail. Total elevation gain is approximately 650 feet. The trail head is right past the bridge that passes over Pipiwai Stream on the mauka side of the highway. The trail winds uphill along the edge of Pipiwai Stream past several waterfalls and pools. The remains

Makahiku Falls

of the beautiful Makahiku Falls. Makahiku Falls cascades a phenomenal 184 feet from one pool into another. The pool at the crest of the falls is sometimes referred to as "Infinity Pool."

When flowing, it is a sight to behold. Unfortunately, it has a tendency to dry up in the summer when there is less rain. There is a small sign noting the location of the falls along the trail. Ask the park rangers about the falls if you want to know about its current flow rates before hiking.

Just beyond the falls you'll encounter a giant banyan tree (*photo on page 66*), a native of India. In another half mile you enter a woodland of mixed ohi'a and koa trees. Continue your hike over foot bridges above the stream and through lush tropical forests of introduced bamboo, mango and guava. Be prepared for rain, mud and slippery mosses.

Because of the marshy ground, wooden boardwalks have been built to make hiking easier. Once you arrive at the bamboo forest, you'll definitely feel like you've stepped into another world.

Despite not being native to Hawai'i, the bamboo is beautiful. More than 30 feet tall, the exotic forest is cool and dark and even quite spooky. The winds that

of a sugar mill dam, irrigation systems and flumes of the late 1800's can be seen in several places along the trail.

Be sure to close any gates you pass through as cattle are permitted to graze inside the fence. Speaking of which, watch out for what the cows may have left behind on the trail.

MAKAHIKU & WAIMOKU FALLS
On Pipiwai Trail - Highway 31
★★★★★

The first half-mile heads up gently sloping meadows to an overlook funnel up from the sea cause the leafy tops of the bamboo to sway, and as the poles below knock together in the gloom, they produce sounds that are both beautiful and eerie, like primitive music.

As you leave the bamboo forest, you can catch a glimpse of 400-foot Waimoku Falls (*photos on page 8 and 15*) taking its long plunge down the face of a horseshoe-shaped cliff into a shallow pool at its base. From here you'll have to cross the streams (their depth and flow rate depend on recent rainfall) to reach the falls.

All said and done, the hike to Waimoku Falls is 4 miles round trip and takes approximately two hours up and an hour and a half down.

Mosquitoes are common here, especially in the wetter winter months. Be sure to bring bottled water if you hike and never drink the stream water (see page 15). Sturdy shoes (or hiking boots) are a must and a hiking pole may prove useful for some hikers. Use extreme caution crossing the streams near Waimoku Falls and do not cross them at all if it has recently rained.

The Pipiwai Trail is one of the best hikes on Maui. Don't miss it!

LINDBERGH'S GRAVE
Mile Marker 41 - Highway 31
★★★☆☆

Our next stop on Highway 31 is the Palapala Ho'omau Church, located 8 miles south of Hana and one mile south of the 'Ohe'o Gulch on the makai side of the highway.

A narrow road around mile marker 41 leads to the church. A small sign pointing left that says "Limited Parking" is tacked on the side of a tree marking the road. Many people miss this spot, but if you keep an eye out for it, you won't be one of them. It's definitely worth a stop.

The famous aviator Charles Lindbergh lies at rest on the tranquil church grounds. Lindbergh died on Aug. 26, 1974 after living his last days on the bountiful Hana coast. Shortly before he died he sketched out a simple design for his grave and coffin. The church was built in 1857 and is actually made out of limestone coral.

Lindbergh's grave is located behind the church under the shade of a Java plum tree. We feel the most beautiful part of this spot is the surrounding scenery. The coastal views down beyond the grave site and gardens are exquisite.

SOUTH KIPAHULU, MOKULAU, & KAUPO
Pi'ilani Highway
Highway 37 to Upcountry

Beyond Lindbergh's grave, the paved road will continue through more rural Maui. Soon you'll notice the road conditions

Charles Lindbergh's Grave

The rugged and undeveloped south east shore is a unique experience all to itself.

deteriorate. This is because the county of Maui does not perform regular maintenance on the roads, and naturally they have become a bit "rough" with age.

Road Closures: We again want to remind you that as of press time, the road is still closed from a half-mile beyond mile marker 40 until you get past Kaupo. The following spots are listed on the chance they'll have the road re-opened by your trip. That said...

Here's what you can expect ahead. From mile marker 40 until 38 the road is about as narrow as it will get for the entire drive ahead - don't fret though, it's not that bad - just drive it slowly and watch out for any blind curves. From mile marker 38 until 33 the road becomes broken pavement and/or gravel, but again, it's not that bad; just keep it slow. While many rental companies say you shouldn't drive this stretch of road (because they don't want to service anyone stuck on it), visitors frequently drive it without incident. The drive down this stretch of road is spectacular enough to make you think you've left the island for another part of the world. Don't let anyone talk you out of making this drive; it is an experience you don't want to leave Maui without. At mile marker 33 you can breathe a sigh of relief because it is all paved again until the end. You can't help but laugh at the road change when you reach it, too (near Manawainui Gulch). We find it humorous every time.

So you're probably wondering what makes this part of the drive so special. What's intriguing about this part of Maui is how different it is from the Hana Highway directly across the island. Haleakala stands between these two halves of the island and the change is nothing short of amazing, a tropical rainforest on one side and prairie grassland and near-desert on the other. It is beautiful on this side of Haleakala though, and you can get some amazing coastal views and a rare look at the back of Haleakala's missing mountain-side that was eroded away in the distant past only to be partially filled again in the more recent (geologically speaking) lava flows.

KIPAHULU COASTLINE
Mile Marker 40 - Highway 31
★★★★☆

If you skipped Lindbergh's Grave, then you'll have one last chance to get a really great view of the Kipahulu coastline. A half-mile past the 40 mile marker this is a very small pullout on the mauka side of the highway. If you head over the road to the ocean, you'll find an incredible view of the coastline. As always, use caution crossing the road here.

KUKUI'ULA FALLS
Mile Marker 39.3 - Highway 31
★★☆☆☆

Just before you reach mile marker 39, Kukui'ula Stream passes under the highway, and up ahead you'll have the opportunity to glimpse yet another beautiful coastal falls.

Viewing it can be a bit tricky. You can't see the falls from the spot where the stream flows under the highway. Instead, as you drive into the first valley, keep your eyes open for the second set of guardrails (after the road turns makai past a beach and up a small hill). Here you should see a small gravel driveway makai side. Pull into this driveway and look back towards the coast. Here you should see Kukui'ula Falls dropping about 40 feet into the ocean. You can't get to the falls, so snap a photo and continue on.

ALELELE TRAIL & FALLS
Mile Marker 39 - Highway 31
★★★☆☆

About 0.3 of a mile past mile marker 39 there is a white bridge with "Alelele" written on the side of it. Here you will notice several trails moving inland towards Alelele Falls. Technically, this area is also

Map continued on page 46

Kalepa
Point

38

Haleakala
National Park

Manawainui Valley

37

← Haleakala
Crater

4,000 ft

Graded gravel road
(Approx. 5 Miles)

31

36

Kaupo Gap

Mokulau

3,000 ft

35

2000 ft

500 ft

Kaupo Trail

Kaupo Store

KAUPO
★

© Copyright 2007. Hawaiian Style Organization, LLC.

1000 ft

34

Waiuha
Bay

Kamanawa Point

Kailio Point

33

Mamalu
Bay

32

Lapehu Point

Waiu
Bay

Koa
Heiau

31

Nu'u
Bay

N

30 31

Pi'ilani Hwy

Huakini
Bay

29

•Note: Be mindful of winds from the south.
It can get extremely windy on the leeward side
of Haleakala. Also note that Road closures in
this area may occur due to danger of rock slides.

Pullout to view
Pokowai Sea Arch

Pokowai Sea Arch

Manawainui
Bridge & Gulch

26

Legend

0   0.5   1 Mile

THE PI'ILANI HIGHWAY

Trail/Path
Ditch/Tunnel
Dirt/Gravel Rd

Map continued on page 60

inside of Haleakala National Park, but most people spend their time at the overcrowded 'Ohe'o Gulch area and never visit this part of the park. Alelele Stream is easy to find, and it is about a 10-minute walk along the trail (and streambed) to get to this falls. There is a pullout on the makai side of the road that leads to a landing where you can park the car. You may have to rock skip a bit and/or cross the stream, but keep heading towards the valley wall where the waterfall is.

This waterfall is lovely, and hardly anybody knows it is here. As is typical with many falls on Maui, in the summertime it may not be flowing. If the weather has been especially dry, you can probably assume as much for the falls and may want to skip this spot.

MOKULAU & KAUPO STORE
Mile Marker 35 - Highway 31

As you travel south along Highway 31, the turn off to Mokulau is just before mile marker 35 (makai side) and before the town of Kaupo. Turn left onto the dirt road leading toward the ocean. You will pass Hui Aloha Church and cemetery. Park along the road and then walk

Kaupo Gap Lookout provides an absolutely incredible view of Haleakala.

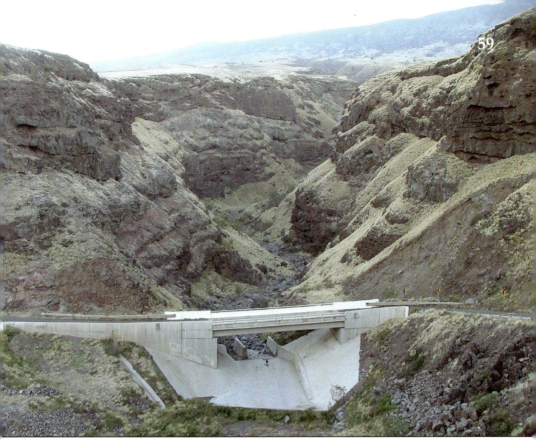

Manawainui Gulch is one of many interesting erosional features of this area.

to the shoreline. From here you can get some of the best views of the southeast Maui coastline. There also are several lava outcroppings in this area.

The Kaupo Store right beyond this stop (past the 35 mile marker) is your last place to pick up snacks before reaching Tedeschi Winery near Highway 37.

KAUPO GAP LOOKOUT
Mile Marker 32 - Highway 31
★★★★☆

Right beyond mile marker 32 is one of the best spots to see the Kaupo Gap, the large valley in the side of Haleakala. Would you believe that is an erosional valley? This is mother nature at work, not geologic forces like those found at Mount St. Helens (a pressurized eruption in 1980).

One thing you certainly won't miss is the wind in this location. When the trades are blowing at a nice pace, it can be some of the strongest wind felt on Maui.

Make sure you get out of the car here and look around; the scenery is awe-inspiring, even just a few steps off the road towards the ocean.

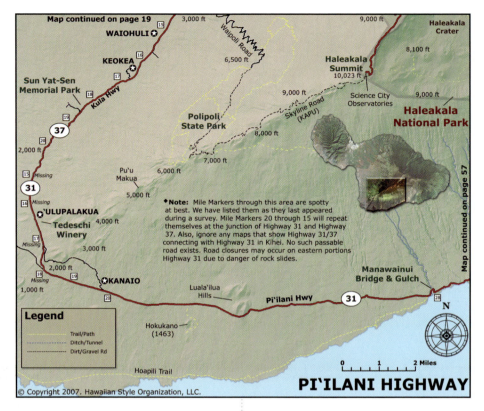

Note: Mile Markers through this area are spotty at best. We have listed them as they last appeared during a survey. Mile Markers 20 through 15 will repeat themselves at the junction of Highway 31 and Highway 37. Also, ignore any maps that show Highway 31/37 connecting with Highway 31 in Kihei. No such passable road exists. Road closures may occur on eastern portions Highway 31 due to danger of rock slides.

© Copyright 2007. Hawaiian Style Organization, LLC.

PI'ILANI HIGHWAY

POKOWAI SEA ARCH
Mile Marker 29 - Highway 31
★★★☆☆

As you continue on Highway 31, beyond mile marker 29, you should see a pull out makai. Here you can view the Pokowai Sea Arch. The arch was formed when flowing lava from the volcano collided with the cold Pacific waters.

MANAWAINUI GULCH
Mile Marker 28 - Highway 31
★★★★☆

Around mile marker 28 on Highway 31 you'll come to Manawainui Bridge, which crosses over a giant gulch. Slightly up the road before crossing the bridge is a good place to stop and takes photographs of this incredible geologic wonder. To appreciate its massive size, let a few vehicles pass by and drive over the bridge in front of you.

As you continue on, you'll likely notice there's not much located in this part of Maui, but if you look around between mile markers 24 and 20 you'll see some ancient Hawaiian ruins. Hawaiians once heavily populated this area, but today it is desolate and dry. However, native Hawaiians are attempting to rebuild the area, known as Kahikinui.

From this point onward you are entering Upcountry Maui and getting closer to Highway 37. But take our word for it: Between here and our next major stop (Sun Yat-Sen Park), there is absolutely nothing to see or do.

Enjoy the scenic highway driving ahead. Part of it even looks like a small roller coaster track for cars, and it is always fun just to drive up and down the large dips. It also is worth noting that ahead of you mile markers 19-15 are only visible coming from the other direction. In fact, several are missing and/or numbered incorrectly.

UPCOUNTRY MAUI
Start of the Haleakala Highway
'Ulupalakua to Kula

TEDESCHI WINERY & RANCH STORE
Mile Marker 15 - Hwy 31/37
★★★☆☆

As you leave the windswept grasslands of south Maui behind you, you'll begin to enter Upcountry Maui. The town of 'Ulupalakua might even sneak up on you, but be sure to give this small town the attention it's due.

'Ulupalakua is best known for our next stop, Tedeschi Vineyards

Upcountry sunsets are phenomenal

and the surrounding 20,000-acre 'Ulupalakua Ranch. Located off Highway 31/37 on the mauka side of the road you'll find the Tedeschi Winery and the Ranch Store.

This is the only commercial winery on the island of Maui. At the winery you can sample their various award-winning wines while enjoying a free tour. A famous pineapple wine, called Maui Blanc, is a popular vintage from Tedeschi Winery. Many folks also like to enjoy samples of Maui Brut Champagne.

The tasting room, located inside a cottage originally built for Hawai'i's King Kalakaua in 1874, is open daily from 9 a.m.-5 p.m.

If the winery isn't enough of a reason to stop, the view is. At more than 2,000 feet above sea level this is a splendid example of what Upcountry Maui has to offer. From this vantage point there are extensive views of both the Central Valley and West Maui Mountains. After Tedeschi Winery, don't forget the mile markers are going to jump back to 20 again heading towards Kula.

Dr. Sun Yat-Sen

SUN YAT-SEN MEMORIAL PARK
Mile Marker 18 - Highway 37
★★★☆☆

Sun Yat-Sen Memorial Park is a small roadside park in Keokea (makai) between mile markers 18 and 19. It is about 2,400 feet above the south Maui coast and scenic views here are excellent.

Who was Sun Yat-Sen? Dr. Sun Yat-Sen (1866-1925) was a revolutionary in China and a political leader who was often referred to as the "father of modern China." Yat-Sen served as the first provisional president when the Republic of China was founded in 1912. He had family and friends in Hawaii and attended college on Oahu. The 'Ulupalakua ranch donated the land for the park in 1989. Today the park features a bronze statue of Yat-Sen along with a few other memorial statues.

From this location you can get spectacular scenic views, including an excellent view of the surrounding Hawaiian Islands offshore: Kaho'olawe (the larger one to the left), uninhabited after decades of use as a bombing range and Molokini (the smaller one in front of Kaho'olawe), a semi-circular island. Its deep cove is a very popular snorkeling spot. Off to your left, near the shoreline, is the Pu'u Ola'i cinder cone in Makena State Park. Ahead of you on the horizon is Lana'i and to your right are the West Maui Mountains, likely draped in clouds.

One last great thing about this vantage point is the incredible sunsets. If you are lucky enough to be at this location late in the day before the sun sets, you will get a color show unlike anything you've ever seen. As the sun sinks over the island of Lana'i it makes for a sunset you'll remember forever (see page 61).

Beyond this park the area begins to become more developed. You may find several small scenic pullouts

Upcountry gardens are definitely worth a stop.

that interest you. As you ease your way back into civilization, around mile marker 14, you'll come to the first of two junctions (southern and northern) of Highways 37 and 377.

At the first (southern) junction stay on Highway 37. We're going to take you to the stops along that route first. When you reach the second (northern) junction, turn mauka onto Highway 377 and then we'll take a look at those stops. The map on page 19 should help clarify this.

ENCHANTING FLORAL GARDENS
Mile Marker 10 – Highway 37
★★★☆☆

Near mile marker 10 on Highway 37 you'll find a sign on the mauka side informing you of our next stop, the Enchanting Floral Gardens. The Enchanting Floral Gardens in Kula has eight acres of walking tours displaying more than 1,500 species of tropical and semi-tropical plants and flowers from around the world. The more you stroll up the path the more rewarding it is.

The garden has a wide variety of exotic flowers such as proteas, orchids, hibiscus, jade vines and a variety of fruit trees. Some have complained the garden is not maintained well, but overall we were pleased with it and found the price of $5 (per adult as of press time) reasonable. They are open 9 a.m. to 5 p.m. daily.

After the garden, keep heading north until you come to the northern junction of Highways 37 and 377. Turn mauka onto Highway 377, the beginning of the Upper Haleakala Highway.

HIGHWAY 378
CRATER ROAD TURN OFF
Mile Marker 6 – Highway 377

Highway 377 is only nine miles long before rejoining with Highway 37, but the first six miles are officially the Upper Haleakala Highway. Right before mile marker 6, you'll find the turn off (mauka) to Highway 378, which is known as Crater Road (also the Haleakala Highway). Highway 378 will take you to the summit of Mount Haleakala and to the remainder of Haleakala National Park. This is a whole day's journey in itself, and you likely won't have time to visit it all with anything less than several (6+) hours to spare.

KULA BOTANICAL GARDENS
Mile Marker 8.5 – Highway 377
★★★☆☆

About half a mile beyond mile marker 8 you'll find our next stop on the mauka side of the road, Kula Botanical Gardens. Kula Botanical Gardens is home to nearly 2,000 species of indigenous Hawaiian flora and fauna. The true king of this garden is the showy protea. However, the plants aren't the

Brilliant protea plants are just some of the wonders of Upcountry gardens.

only thing to see at Kula Botanical Gardens. There also are some great views from their reception center. A stream and koi pond can also be found within the six-acre garden.

The garden is open Monday-Saturday from 9 a.m. until 4 p.m. and admission is $7.50 for adults, $2 for children 6 to 12 and under 6 is free.

www.KulaBotanicalGarden.com

POLIPOLI SPRINGS STATE PARK
Mile Marker 9 – Highway 377
★★★☆☆

Right before mile marker 9 on Highway 377, mauka side, you'll see the turn off for Waipoli Road.

Waipoli Road includes several switchbacks up the side of Haleakala to Polipoli Springs State Park, an infrequently visited but very beautiful state park on Maui.

Polipoli Springs State Park is around 6,200 feet above sea level in the Kula Forest Reserve and encompasses nearly 10 acres of recreational area. This Upcountry park offers amazing views of both Maui below and the neighboring islands of Lana'i and Kaho'olawe. The towering trees, mature forest of redwoods, and other exotic native vegetation species such as plum, cypress, sugi and ash are highlights of the park. Several trails also are available. Since the road is only partially paved, and the rest merely graded dirt and gravel, it is recommended mostly for 4-wheel-drive vehicles.

However, the first part of the drive should be quite accessible and you can walk the rest of the way if you're feeling up to a hiking challenge. A light jacket might also be a good idea as it can become quite chilly. If you decide to skip this stop, you'll soon find yourself back at the southern junction of Highway 37/377.

We should note that in Feb. 2007, Polipoli State Park had several brush fires that closed the park. However, according to the Hawaii Department of Forestry Polipoli Springs is now reopened to the public.

From here where you go next is up to you. Aloha for using our guide to the Hana Highway & Beyond.

If you are looking for additional information on this drive, please visit our Web site listed below. On those pages we've included pictures of everything described in this guide along with any updates and/or corrections.

Visit us online for:

Photography, posters, calendars, stickers, apparel, maps, and much more...

www.HawaiianStyle.org

Banyan trees, such as this one on the Pipiwai Trail, are a trademark of Hawai'i.

Hana Highway - Mile by Mile

INDEX

INDEX

INDEX